120

Portrait Paintings

CD-ROM and Book

Edited by
Carol Belanger Grafton

Dover Publications, Inc.
Mineola, New York

The CD-ROM in this book contains all of the images. Each image has been saved in 300-dpi high-resolution and 72-dpi Internet-ready JPEG formats. There is no installation necessary. Just insert the CD into your computer and call the images into your favorite software (refer to the documentation with your software for further instructions).

Within the Images folder on the CD, you will find two additional folders—"High Resolution JPG" and "JPG." Every image has a unique file name in the following format: xxx.JPG. The first 3 digits of the file name correspond to the number printed under the image in the book. The last 3 characters of the file name, "JPG," refer to the file format. So, 001.JPG would be the first file in the folder.

Also included on the CD-ROM is Dover Design Manager, a simple graphics editing program for Windows that will allow you to view, print, crop, and rotate the images.

For technical support, contact:
Telephone: 1 (617) 249-0245
Fax: 1 (617) 249-0245
Email: dover@artimaging.com
Internet: **http://www.dovertechsupport.com**
The fastest way to receive technical support is via email or the Internet.

Bibliographical Note

120 Portrait Paintings CD-ROM and Book, is a new work, first published by Dover Publications, Inc., in 2007.

Dover Electronic Clip Art®

International Standard Book Number: 0-486-99835-5

Manufactured in the United States of America
Dover Publications, Inc., 31 East 2nd Street, Mineola, N.Y. 11501

002. Sofonisba Anguissola
Self-Portrait; 1556

001. Alessandro Allori
Self-Portrait; 1555

004. POMPEO BATONI
Thomas William Coke; 1774

003. GIUSEPPE ARCIMBOLDO
Rudolph II as "Vertumnus"; 1590

006. CECILIA BEAUX
Man with the Cat (Henry Sturgis Drinker); 1898

005. FRÉDÉRIC BAZILLE
Self-Portrait; 1867–68

008. Giovanni Bellini
Portrait of Doge Leonardo Loredan; 1501–05

007. Max Beckman
Self-Portrait Dressed as a Clown; 1921

010. GIOVANNI BOLDINI
Count Robert de Montesquiou-Fezensac; 1897

009. MARIE-GUILLEMINE BENOIST
Portrait of a Negress; 1799–1800

012. FRANÇOIS BOUCHER
A Landscape Painter in His Studio; 1753

011. SANDRO BOTTICELLI
Profile of a Young Woman; 1480

014. AGNOLO BRONZINO
Bia de' Medici; ca. 1541

013. DIERIC BOUTS
Portrait of a Man (Jan van Winckele?); 1462

016. GUSTAVE CAILLEBOTTE
Self-Portrait; ca. 1892

015. HORACE BUNDY
Vermont Lawyer; 1841

018. ROSALBA CARRIERA
Louis XV, as Dauphin; 1720–21

017. ROBERT CAMPIN
Portrait of a Woman; ca. 1430

020. PAUL CÉZANNE
Madame Cézanne in the Conservatory; 1891–92

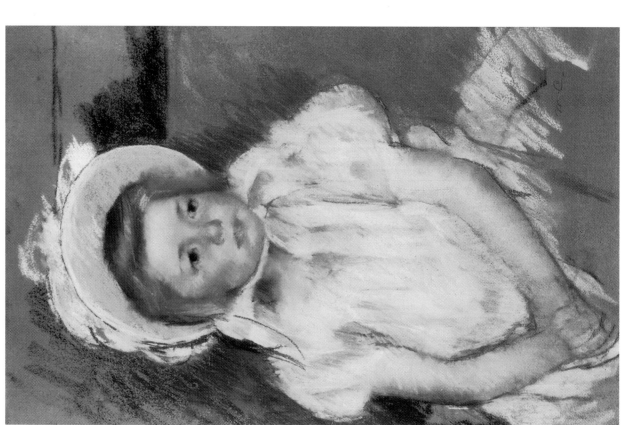

019. MARY CASSATT
Simone in a White Bonnet; 1901

021. Philippe de Champaigne
Triple Portrait of Cardinal Richelieu; 1642

022. Jean-Baptiste-Siméon Chardin
Self-Portrait; 1779

023. WILLIAM MERRITT CHASE
Portrait of Miss Dora Wheeler; 1883

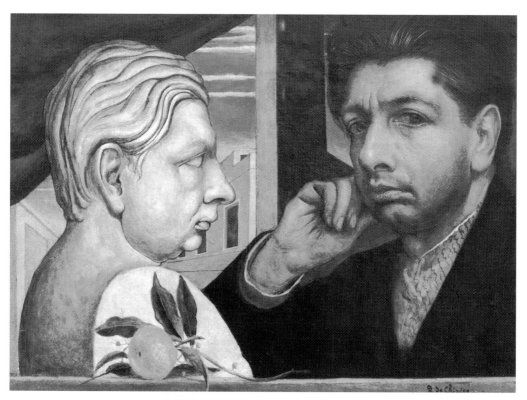

024. GIORGIO DE CHIRICO
Self-Portrait; 1922

026. JEAN CLOUET
Francois I; 1520–25

025. PETRUS CHRISTUS
Portrait of a Lady; 1470

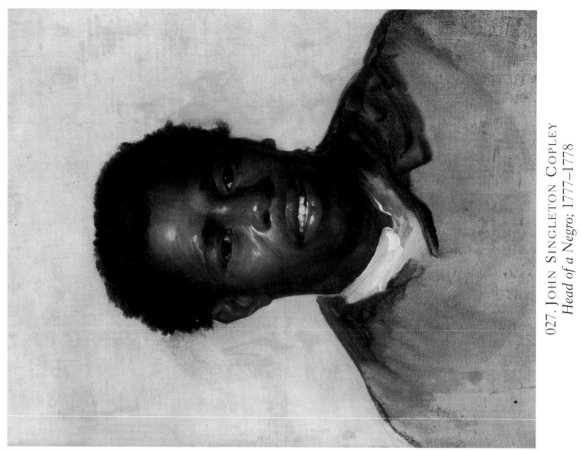

028. LOVIS CORINTH
Self-Portrait with Skeleton; 1896–97

030. ANTONIO ALLEGRI (called CORREGGIO)
Self-Portrait; 1510

029. JEAN-BAPTISTE-CAMILLE COROT
The Woman with the Pearl; 1858–68

032. KENYON COX
Portrait of Maxfield Parrish; 1905

031. GUSTAVE COURBET
Portrait of the Artist (called Man with a Pipe); 1848–49

034. WALTER CRANE
Self-Portrait; 1912

033. LUCAS CRANACH THE ELDER
Portrait of Dr. Johannes Cuspinian; 1502

035. GERARD DAVID
Portrait of a Goldsmith; 1505–1510

036. EDGAR DEGAS
Madame Théodore Gobillard (née Yves Morisot); 1869

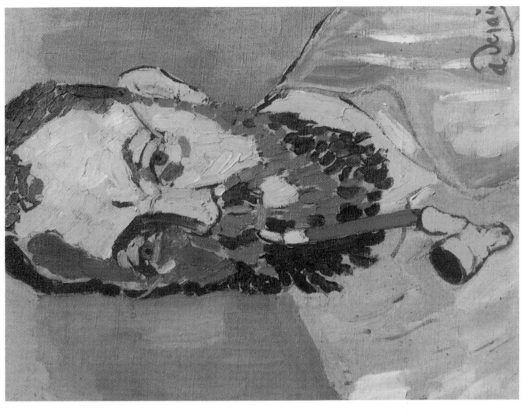

038. ANDRÉ DERAIN
Portrait of Matisse; 1905

037. EUGÈNE DELACROIX
Self-Portrait; 1839

040. ALBRECHT DÜRER
Self-Portrait; 1498

039. OTTO DIX
Self-Portrait; 1912

042. THOMAS EAKINS
Portrait of Walt Whitman; 1887–88

041. ANTHONY VAN DYCK
Family Portrait; 1621

044. THOMAS GAINSBOROUGH
The Blue Boy; 1770

043. JAN VAN EYCK
Arnolfini Wedding Portrait; 1434

046. ARTEMISIA GENTILESCHI
Self-Portrait Playing the Lute; 1615–17

045. PAUL GAUGUIN
Portrait of Mette Gauguin, the Aritist's Wife; 1884

048. ALBERTO GIACOMETTI
Self-Portrait; 1921

047. DOMENICO GHIRLANDAIO
Portrait of Giovanna Tornabuoni; 1488

050. WILLIAM GLACKENS
Portrait of Ernest Lawson; 1911

049. ANNE-LOUIS GIRODET DE ROUSSY-TRIOSON
Portrait of Mustapha; 1819

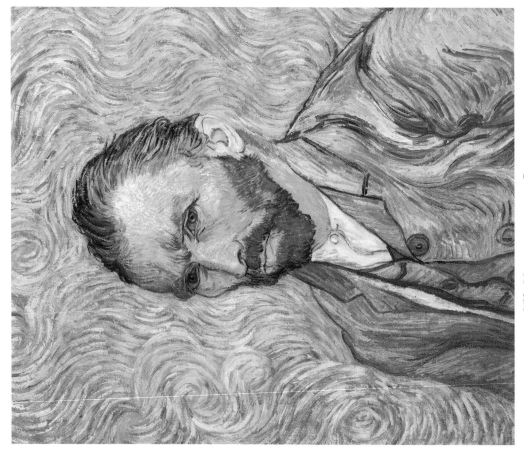

052. Vincent van Gogh
Self-Portrait; 1889

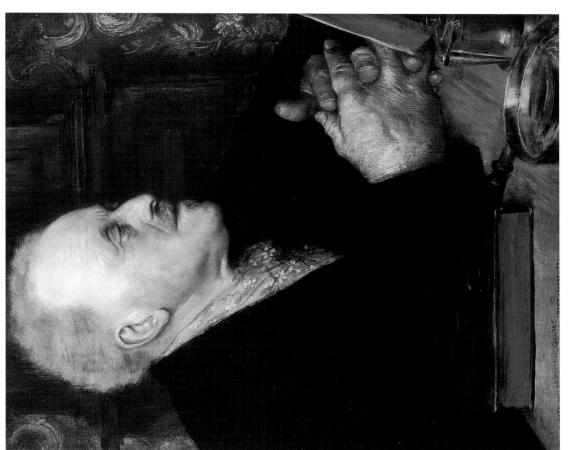

051. Norbert Goeneutte
Dr. Paul Gachet; 1891

054. Frans Hals
Portrait of a Young Man with a Skull; 1626

053. Francisco de Goya
Portrait of Doña Isabel de Porcel; 1805

056. NICHOLAS HILLIARD
Queen Elizabeth I; 1575

055. ROBERT HENRI
Grace—Chinese Girl; 1917

058. HANS HOLBEIN THE YOUNGER
Portrait of Erasmus of Rotterdam; 1523

057. WILLIAM HOGARTH
Self-Portrait with his Dog, Trump; 1745

060. EDWARD HOPPER
Self-Portrait; 1925–30

059. MILTON WILLIAM HOPKINS
Pierrepont Edward Lacey and His Dog, Gun; 1832

062. HENRY INMAN
Sequoyah (after a painting by Charles Bird King); 1830

061. JEAN INGRES
M. Marcotte; 1810

064. ANGELICA KAUFFMANN
Self-Portrait with the Bust of Minerva; 1780

063. FRIDA KAHLO
Self-Portrait with Monkey; 1938

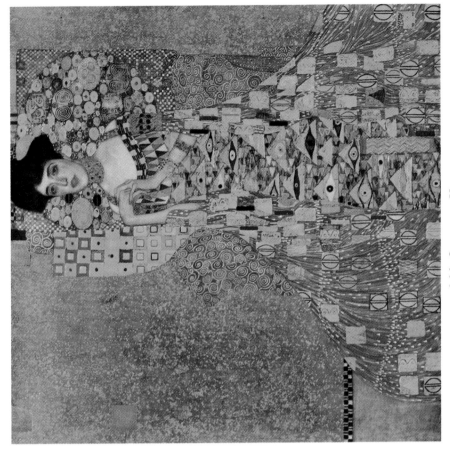

066. GUSTAV KLIMT
Portrait of Adele Bloch-Bauer I; 1907

065. ERNST LUDWIG KIRCHNER
Self-Portrait as a Soldier; 1915

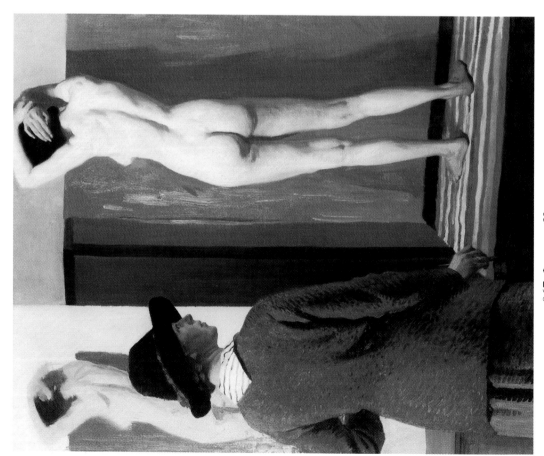

067. Laura Knight
Self-Portrait; 1913

068. Nicholas de Largillière
Elizabeth Throckmorton; 1729

070. SIR THOMAS LAWRENCE
Portrait of Mrs. Robert Burne-Jones

069. MAURICE QUENTIN DE LA TOUR
Self-Portrait; 1735

072. LEONARDO DA VINCI
Mona Lisa; 1503–06

071. SIR PETER LELY
Portrait of Hon. Mary Wharton

074. Jean-Étienne Liotard
Self-Portrait; 1744–45

073. Judith Leyster
Self-Portrait at the Easel; 1630

076. EDWARD GREEN MALBONE
Eliza Izard (Mrs. Thomas Pinckney Jr.); 1801

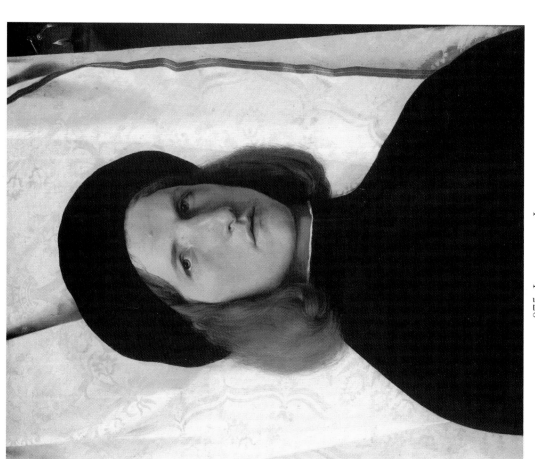

075. LORENZO LOTTO
Young Man Before a White Curtain; 1506–08

078. QUENTIN MASSYS
Portrait of a Notary; 1510

077. ÉDOUARD MANET
Berthe Morisot with a Bouquet of Violets; 1872

080. Sir John Everett Millais
Sweet Emma Morland; 1892

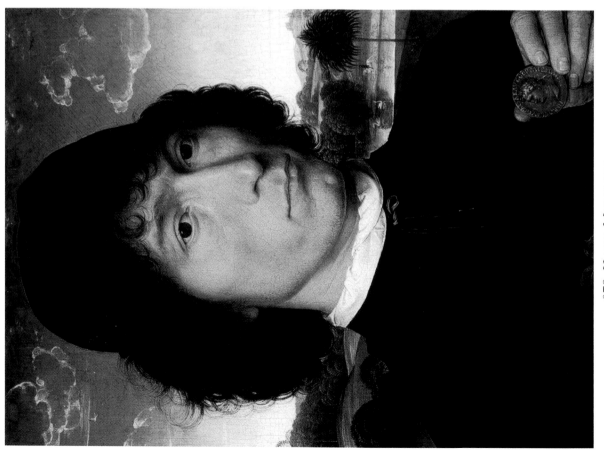

079. Hans Memling
*Portrait of a Man with a Coin of the Emperor Nero
(Bernard Bembo?); 1473–74*

082. CLAUDE MONET
Self-Portrait; 1886

081. AMEDEO MODIGLIANI
Self-Portrait; 1919

084. GIOVANNI BATTISTA MORONI
Don Gabriel de la Cueva, Duke of Albuquerque; 1560

083. BERTHE MORISOT
Portrait of Jeanne Pontillon; 1894

086. PARMIGIANINO
(Girolamo Francesco Maria Mazzola)
Self-Portrait in a Convex Mirror; 1524

085. EDVARD MUNCH
Self-Portrait Against Red Background; 1906

088. Pietro Perugino
Francesco delle Opere; 1494

087. Rembrandt Peale
Rubens Peale with a Geranium; 1801

090. PABLO PICASSO
Gertrude Stein; 1906

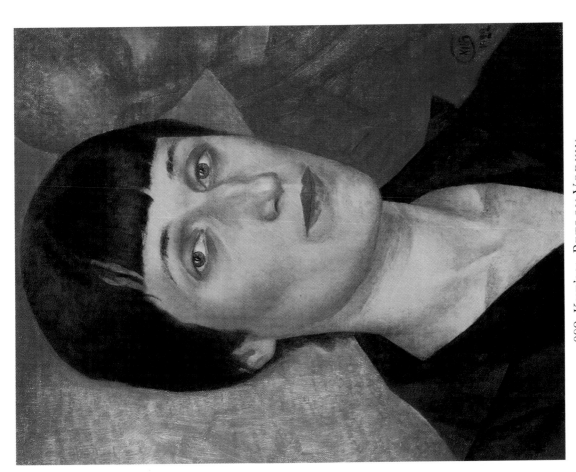

089. KUZ'MA PETROV-VODKIN
Portrait of the Poet Anna Akhmatova; 1922

092. CAMILLE PISSARRO
Portrait of Cézanne; 1874

091. PIERRO DELLA FRANCESCA
Portrait of Battista Sforza; 1465

094. JACOPO PONTORMO
Lady in a Red Dress; 1532–33

093. PIERO DEL POLLAIUOLO
Portrait of a Woman; 1441–42

096. NICOLAS POUSSIN
Self-Portrait; 1650

095. ROCKWELL KENT
Cândido Portinari; 1937

098. REMBRANDT VAN RIJN
Self-Portrait; 1640

097. RAPHAEL (Raphael Santi)
Portrait of a Young Woman (Lady with a Unicorn); 1505–06

100. DIEGO RIVERA
Elisa Saldivar de Gutiérrez Roldán; 1946

099. PIERRE-AUGUSTE RENOIR
Mlle. Irène Cahen d'Anvers; 1880

102. Dante Gabriel Rossetti
Il Ramoscello (Bella e Buona); 1865

101. George Romney
Portrait of Emma, Lady Hamilton; 1786

104. PETER PAUL RUBENS
Portrait of Suzanne Fourment; 1625

103. HENRI ROUSSEAU
Myself: Portrait Landscape; 1890

105. JOHN SINGER SARGENT
Lady Agnew of Lochnaw; 1892–93

106. GEORGE SCHOLZ
Self-Portrait in Front of an Advertising Column; 1926

108. LUCA SIGNORELLI
Middle-Aged Man; 1500

107. JAN VAN SCOREL
The Schoolboy; 1531

110. JAMES TISSOT
Portrait de Mlle. L.L...(Jeune Femme en Veste Rouge); 1864

109. GILBERT STUART
George Washington; 1796

112. Henry de Toulouse-Lautrec
Gustave Lucien Dennery; 1883

111. Titian (Tiziano Vecelli)
Flora; 1514

114. JAN VERMEER
Girl with a Pearl Earring; 1665–66

113. DIEGO VELAZQUÉZ
Infanta Margarita Therese; 1658–60

115. ÉLISABETH VIGÉE-LEBRUN
Self-Portrait; 1782

116. ÉDOUARD VUILLARD
Portrait of Théodore Duret; 1912

118. JAMES ABBOTT MCNEILL WHISTLER
Portrait of the Artist's Mother; 1871

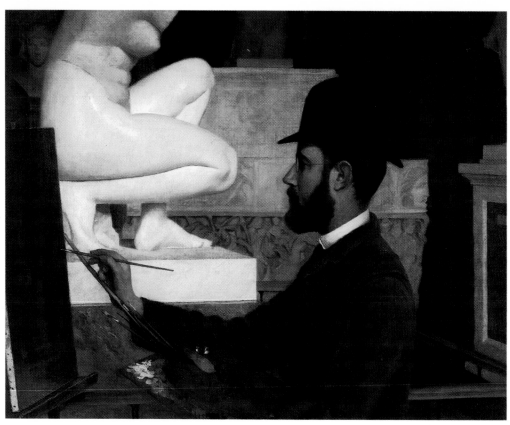

119. WILLIAM J. WHITTEMORE
Portrait of Charles C. Curran; 1888

120. JOHANN ZOFFANY
Francis I; 1770

List of Works

001. Alessandro Allori; *Self Portrait*; 1555

002. Sofonisba Anguissola; *Self Portrait*; 1556; oil on canvas; 22" x 26" (66 x 57 cm)

003. Giuseppe Arcimboldo; *Rudolph II as "Vertumnus"*; 1590; oil on panel; 27⅞" x 22⅝" (70.5 x 57.5 cm)

004. Pompeo Batoni; *Thomas William Coke;* 1774; oil on canvas; 97" x 67" (246 x 170 cm)

005. Frédéric Bazille; *Self Portrait*; 1867–68; oil on canval; 21⅜" x 18¼" (54.6 x 46.4 cm)

006. Cecilia Beaux; *Man with the Cat (Henry Sturgis Drinker)*; 1898; oil on canvas; 48" x 34½" (121.9 x 87.8 cm)

007. Max Beckman; *Self Portrait Dressed as a Clown*; 1921; oil on canvas; 39⅜" x 23¼" in (100 x 59 cm)

008. Giovanni Bellini; *Portrait of Doge Leonardo Loredan*; 1501-1505; tempera on wood; 24⅜" x 17¾" (62 x 45 cm)

009. Marie Guillemine Benoist; *Portrait of a Negress*; 1799–1800; oil on canvas; 31⅞" x 25½" (81 x 65 cm)

010. Giovanni Boldini; *Count Robert de Montesquiou-Fezensac*; 1897; oil on canvas; 65⅜" x 32¼" (166 x 82 cm)

011. Sandro Botticelli; *Profile of a Young Woman*; 1480; oil on panel; 18¾" x 15" (47.5 x 35 cm)

012. Francois Boucher; *A Landscape Painter in His Studio*; 1753; oil on wood; 10⅝" x 8⅝" (27 x 22 cm)

13. Dieric Bouts; *Portrait of a Man*; 1462; oil on wood; 12¼" x 7⅞" (31 x 20 cm)

14. Agnolo Bronzino; *Bia de'Medici*; ca. 1541; tempera on panel; 23¼" x 17¾" (59 x 45 cm)

15. Horace Bundy; *Vermont Lawyer*; 1841; oil on canvas; 44" x 35½" (111.8 x 90.3 cm)

16. Gustave Caillebotte; *Self-Portrait*; ca. 1892; oil on canvas; 16" x 13" (40.5 x 32.5 cm)

17. Robert Campin; *Portrait of a Woman*; ca.1430; oil on wood 16⅛" x 11" (41 x 28 cm)

18. Rosalba Carriera; *Louis XV, as Dauphin*; 1720–21; pastel on paper; 20" x 15 " (50.5 x 38.5 cm)

9. Mary Cassatt; *Simone in a White Bonnet*; 1901; pastel on paper; 25⅜" x 16½" (64.7 x 41.9 cm)

20. Paul Cézanne; *Madame Cézanne in the Conservatory*; 1891–92; oil on canvas; 36¼" x 28¾" (92.2 x 73.2 cm)

1. Philippe de Champaigne; *Triple Portrait of Cardinal Richelieu*; 1642; oil on canvas; 22¾" x 28½" (58 x 72 cm)

2. Joshua Reynolds; *Self Portrait*; 1747–49; oil on canvas; 25 x 29¼" (63.5 x 74.3 cm)

3. William Merritt Chase; Portrait of Miss Dora Wheeler; 1883; oil on canvas; 62½" x 65⅛" (158.8 x 165.2 cm)

4. Giorgio de Chirico; *Self Portrait*; 1922; oil on canvas; 15¼" x 20⅛" (38.5 x 51 cm)

5. Petrus Christus; Portrait of a Lady; 1470; oil on wood; 11 x 8¼" (28 x 21 cm)

6) Jean Clouet; *Francois I*; 1520–25; oil on panel; 37⅞" x 29⅛" (96 x 74 cm)

7. John Singleton Copley; *Head of a Negro;* 1777–1778; oil on canvas; 21" x 16¼" (53.3 x 41.3 cm)

8. Lovis Corinth; *Self Portrait with Skeleton*; 1896–97; oil on canvas; 26 x 33⅞" (66 x 86 cm)

9. Jean-Baptiste-Camille Corot; *The Woman with the Pearl*; 1858–68; oil on canvas; 27⅝" x 21¾" (70 x 55 cm)

. Antonio Allegri (called Correggio); *Self Portrait*; 1510; oil on wood; 23¼" x 17⅜" (59 x 44.3 cm)

031. Gustave Courbet; *Portrait of the Artist* (called *Man with a Pipe*); 1848–49; oil on canvas; 17¾" x 14⅝" (45 x 37 cm)

032. Kenyon Cox; *Portrait of Maxfield Parrish*; 1905; oil on canvas; 30" x 25" (76.2 x 63.5 cm)

033. Lucas Cranach the Elder; *Portrait of Dr. Johannes Cuspinian*; 1502; oil on wood; 23¼" x 17¾" (59 x 45 cm)

034. Walter Crane; *Self Portrait*; 1912; oil on canvas; 35¾" x 27" (91 x 68.5 cm)

035. Gerard David; *Portrait of a Goldsmith*; 1505–1510

036. Edgar Degas; *Madame Théodore Gobillard (née Yves Morisot)*; 1869; oil on canvas, 21¾" x 25⅝" (55.2 x 65.1 cm)

037. Eugéne Delacroix; *Self Portrait*; 1839; oil on canvas; 25⅝" x 21½" (65 x 54.5 cm)

038. André Derain; *Portrait of Matisse*; 1905; oil on canvas; 18⅛" x 13¾" (46 x 35 cm)

039. Otto Dix; *Self Portrait*; 1912; oil and tempera on wood; 29" x 19½" (73.6 x 49.5 cm)

040. Albrecht Durer; *Self Portrait*; 1498; oil on panel; 20½" x 16⅛" (52 x 41 cm)

041. Anthony van Dyck; *Family Portrait*; 1621; oil on canvas; 44¾" x 36¾" (17.6 x 14.5 cm)

042. Thomas Eakins; *Portrait of Walt Whitman*; 1887–88; oil on canvas; 30⅛" x 24¼" (76.5 x 61.8 cm)

043. Jan van Eyck; *Arnolfini Wedding Portrait*; 1434; oil on wood; 32¼" x 23½" (81.8 x 59.7 cm)

044. Thomas Gainsborough; *The Blue Boy*; 1770; oil on canvas; 46½" x 48" (118 x 122 cm)

045. Paul Gauguin; *Portrait of Mette Gauguin, the Artist's Wife*; 1884; oil on canvas; 25⅝" x 21¼" (65.1 x 54 cm)

046. Artemisia Gentileschi; *Self Portrait Playing the Lute*; 1615–17; oil on canvas; 30½" x 28¼" (77.5 x 71.8 cm)

047. Domenico Ghirlandaio; *Portrait of Giovanna Tornabuoni*; 1488; tempera on panel; 30¼" x 19¼" (77 x 49 cm)

048. Alberto Giacometti; *Self Portrait*; 1921; oil on canvas; 32¼" x 27⅜" (82.5 x 69.5 cm)

049. Anne-Louis Girodet de Roussy-Trioson; *Portrait of Mustapha*; 1819; oil on canas; 22" x 18⅛" (56 x 46 cm)

050. William Glackens; *Portrait of Ernest Lawson*; 1911; oil on masonite; 30" x 25" (76.3 x 63.6 cm)

051. Norbert Goeneutte; *Dr. Paul Gachet*; 1891; 13¾" x 10⅝" (35 x 27 cm)

052. Vincent van Gogh; *Self Portrait*; 1889; oil on canvas; 25⅝" x 21½" (65 x 54.5 cm)

053. Francisco de Goya; *Portrait of Dona Isabel de Porcel*; 1805; oil on canvas; 32¼" x 21½" (82 x 54.6 cm)

054. Frans Hals; *Portrait of a Young Man with Skull*; 1626; oil on canvas; 36¼" x 31⅞" (92 x 81 cm)

055. Robert Henri; *Grace—Chinese Girl*; 1917; oil on canvas; 24" x 20" (61 x 50.8 cm)

056. Nicholas Hilliard; *Queen Elizabeth I*; 1575; oil on wood; 31⅛" x 24" (79 x 61 cm)

057. Édouard Manet; *Émile Zola*; 1867–68; oil on canvas; 57½" x 44⅞" (146 x 114 cm)

058. Hans Holbein the Younger; *Portrait of Erasmus of Rotterdam*; 1523; oil on wood; 29" x 20¼" (73.6 x 51.4 cm)

059. Milton William Hopkins; *Pierrepont Edward Lacey and His Dog, Gun*; 1832; oil on canvas; 42" x 30" (106.7 x 76.6 cm)

060. Edward Hooper; *Self Portrait*; 1925–30; oil on canvas; 25" x 20⅜" (63.4 x 51.7 cm)

061. JEAN INGRES; *M. Marcotte*; 1810; oil on canvas; 36¾" x 27¼" (93.5 x 69.3 cm)

062. HENRY INMAN; *Sequoyah* (after a painting by Charles Bird King); 1830, oil on canvas; 30⅛" x 25" (76.6 x 63.5 cm)

063. FRIDA KAHLO; *Self Portrait with Monkey*; 1938; oil on masonite; 16" x 12" (40.6 x 30.5 cm)

064. ANGELICA KAUFFMANN; *Self Portrait with the Bust of Minerva*; 1780; oil on canvas; 36⅝" x 30⅛" (93 x 76.5 cm)

065. ERNST LUDWIG KIRCHNER; *Self Portrait as a Soldier*; 1915; oil on canvas; 27¼" x 24" (69 x 61 cm)

066. GUSTAV KLIMT; *Portrait of Adele Bloch-Bauer I*; 1907; oil on canvas; 54¼" x 54¼" (138 x 138 cm)

067. LAURA KNIGHT; *Self Portrait*; 1913; oil on canvas; 60" x 50¼" (152.4 x 127.6 cm)

068. NICOLAS DE LARGILLIÉRE; *Elizabeth Throckmorton*; 1729; oil on canvas; 31⅞" x 26" (81 x 66 cm)

069. MAURICE QUENTIN DE LA TOUR; *Self Portrait*; 1735; pastel on paper; 24¼" x 19⅞" (61.5 x 50.5 cm)

070. SIR THOMAS LAWRENCE; *Portrait of Mrs. Robert Burne-Jones*

071. SIR PETER LELY; *Portrait of Hon Mary Wharton*; 1660; oil on canvas; 50½" x 40½" (128.2 x 102.8 cm)

072. LEONARDO DA VINCI; *Mona Lisa*; 1503–06; oil on panel; 30¼" x 20⅞" (77 x 53 cm)

073. JUDITH LEYSTER; *Self Portrait at the Easel*; 1630; oil on canvas; 29¼" x 25⅝" (74.6 x 65.1 cm)

074. JEAN-ÉTIENNE LIOTARD; *Self Portrait*; 1744–45; pastel on paper; 23⅞" x 18¼" (60.5 x 46.5 cm)

075. LORENZO LOTTO; *Young Man Before a White Curtain*; 1506–08; oil on canvas; 21" x 16¾" (53.3 x 42.3 cm)

076. EDWARD GREEN MALBONE; *Eliza Izard (Mrs. Thomas Pinckney Jr.)*; 1801; watercolor on ivory; 3" x 2¼" (7.4 x 5.8 cm)

077. ÉDOUARD MANET; *Berthe Morisot with a Bouquet of Violets*; 1872; 21½" x 15" (55 x 38 cm)

078. QUENTIN MASSYS; *Portrait of a Notary*; 1510; oil on panel; 31½" x 25⅜" (80 x 64.5 cm)

079) HANS MEMLING; *Portrait of a Man with a Coin of the Emperor Nero*; 1473–74; oil on panel; 12¼" x 9⅛" (31 x 23.2 cm)

080. SIR JOHN EVERETT MILLAIS; *Sweet Emma Morland*; 1892; oil on canvas; 47¾" x 35⅝" (121.3 x 90.8 cm)

081. AMEDEO MODIGLIANI; *Self Portrait*; oil on canvas; 41¼" x 39⅜" (105 x 100 cm)

082. CLAUDE MONET; *Self Portrait*; 1886; oil on canvas; 22" x 15½" (55.9 x 47 cm)

083. BERTHE MORISOT; *Portrait of Jeanne Pontillon*; 1894; oil on canvas; 45¾" x 32" (116 x 81 cm)

084. GIOVANNI BATTISTA MORONI; *Don Gabriel de la Cueva, Duke of Albuquerque*; 1560; 45" x 35¾" (114.5 x 90.8 cm)

085. EDVARD MUNCH; *Self Portrait Against Red Background*; 1906; oil on canvas; 47" x 27¾" (119.5 x 70.5 cm)

086. PARMIGIANINO (Girolamo Francesco Maria Mazzola); *Self Portrait in a Convex Mirror*; 1524; oil on wood; diameter 9⅝" (24.4 cm)

087. REMBRANDT PEALE; *Rubens Peale with a Geranium*; 1801; oil on canvas; 28¼" x 24" (71.7 x 61 cm)

088. PIETRO PERUGINO; *Francesco delle Opere*; 1494; tempera on wood; 20½" x 17¼" (52 x 44 cm)

089. KUZ'MA PETROV-VODKIN; *Portrait of the Poet Anna Akhmatova*; 1922; oil on canvas; 21½" x 17⅛" (54.5 x 43.5 cm)

090. PABLO PICASSO; *Gertrude Stein*; 1906; oil on canvas; 39⅜" x 32" (100.1 x 81.3 cm)

091. PIERRO DELLA FRANCESCA; *Portrait of Battista Aforza*; 1465; tempera on panel; 18½" x 13" (47 x 33 cm)

092. CAMILLE PISSARRO; *Portrait of Cezanne*; 1874; oil on canvas; 28¾" x 23½" (73 x 59.7 cm)

093. PIERO DEL POLLAIUOLO; *Portrait of a Woman*; 1441–42; tempera on wood; 19¼" x 13⅞" (48.9 x 35.2 cm)

094. JACOPO PNTORMO; *Lady in a Red Dress*; 1532–33; oil on panel; 35¼" x 27¾" (89.7 x 70.5 cm)

095. ROCKWELL KENT; *Candido Portinari*; 1937; oil on canvas; 21⅝" x 18" (55 x 46 cm)

096. NICOLAS POUSSIN; *Self Portrait*; 1650; oil on canvas; 38½" x 29⅛" (98 x 74 cm)

097. RAPHAEL SANTI; *Portrait of a Young Woman (Lady with a Unicorn)*; 1505–1506; oil on panel; 26" x 20" (65 x 61 cm)

098. REMBRANDT VAN RIJN; *Self Portrait*; 1640; oil on canvas; 35⅜" x 29½" (90 x 75 cm)

099. PIERRE-AUGUSTE RENOIR; *Mlle. Irène Cahen d'Anvers*; 1880; oil on canvas; 25⅜" x 21¼" (64.3 x 54.1 cm)

100. DIEGO RIVERA; *Elisa Saldivar de Gutiérrez Roldán*; 1946; oil on canvas; 59" x 49¼" (150 x 125 cm)

101. GEORGE ROMNEY; *Portrait of Emma*; Lady Hamilton; 1786

102. DANTE GABRIEL ROSSETTI; *Il Ramoscello (Bella e Buona)*; 1865; oil on canvas; 18⅝" x 15½" (47.6 x 39.4 cm)

103. HENRI ROUSSEAU; *Myself: Portrait Landscape*; 1890; oil on canvas; 56¼" x 43¼" (143 x 110 cm)

104. PETER PAUL RUBENS; *Portrait of Suzanne Fourment*; 1625; oil on oak; 31⅛" x 21¼" (79 x 54 cm)

105. JOHN SINGER SARGENT; *Lady Agnew of Lochnaw*; 1892–93; oil on canvas; 49" x 39¼" (124.5 x 99.7 cm)

106. GEORGE SCHOLTZ; *Self-Portrait in Front of an Advertising Column*; 1926; oil on pasteboard; 23⅝" x 30⅝" (60 x 77.8 cm)

107. JAN VAN SCOREL; *The Schoolboy*; 1531; oil on panel; 18¼" x 13¾" (46.6 x 35 cm)

108. LUCA SIGNORELLI; *Middle Aged Man*; 1500; oil on panel; 19¾" x 12⅝" (50 x 32 cm)

109. GILBERT STUART; *George Washington*; 1796; oil on canvas; 47¾" x 37" (121.3 x 94 cm)

110. JAMES TISSOT; *Portrait de Mlle. L. L. …(Jeune Femme en Veste Rouge)*; 1864; oil on canvas; 48⅞" x 39⅛" (124 x 99.5 cm)

111. TITIAN (Tiziano Vecelli); *Flora*; 1514; oil on canvas; 31½" x 25" (80 x 63.5 cm)

112. HENRY TOULOUSE LAUTREC; *Gustave Lucien Dennery*; 1883; oil on canvas; 21¾" x 18⅛" (55 x 46 cm)

113. DIEGO VELAZQUÉZ; *Infanta Marguarite Therese*; 1654; oil on canvas; 50½" x 39¼" (128.5 x 100 cm)

114. JAN VERMEER; *Girl with a Pearl Earring*; 1665–66; oil on canvas; 17½" x 15⅜" (44.5 x 39 cm)

115. ÉLIZABETH VIGÉE-LEBRUN; *Self Portrait*; 1782; oil on canvas; 39⅜" x 28¾" (100 x 73 cm)

116. ÉDOUARD VUILLARD; *Portrait of Théodore Duret*; 1912; oil on cardboard; 37⅜" x 29½" (95 x 75 cm)

117. ROGIER VAN DER WEYDEN; *Portrait of a Lady*; 1460; oil on oak panel; 13⅜" x 10" (34 x 25.5 cm)

118. JAMES ABBOT McNEILL WHISTLER; *Portrait of the Artist's Mother*; 1871; oil on canvas; 56¾" x 63¾" (144 x 162 cm)

119. WILLIAM J. WHITTEMORE; *Portrait of Charles C. Curran*; 1888; oil on canvas; 17" x 21½" (43.5 x 54.6 cm)

120. JOHANN ZOFFANY; *Francis I*; 1770